GOSPEL CENTERED LIFE

Becoming the person God wants you to be

Steve Timmis and Tim Chester

Gospel-centered life

This US edition first published in 2012. Reprinted 2018.

The Good Book Company
Tel: 866 244 2165
Email: admin@thegoodbook.com

Websites:
N America: www.thegoodbook.com
UK: www.thegoodbook.co.uk
Australia: www.thegoodbook.com.au
New Zealand: www.thegoodbook.co.nz

ISBN: 9781908317766

Cover design by Steve Devane
Printed in Turkey

CONTENTS

PART ONE

GOSPEL CENTERED CHANGE

1 A LIFE FOR GOD

Principle

It's not about me—it's about God and His glory.

Consider this

John walked through the factory gates. The prospect of yet another shift filled him with dread. There are only so many plastic widgets you can churn out, day after day. He knew his prospects weren't good. Walking into a new job was as likely as joining an expedition to Antarctica. He couldn't help wondering if this was all he had to look forward to.

During his first break he sat quietly by himself and watched as his co-workers went about their routine. He thought briefly about what was discussed at the Bible study the night before, where they talked about life being all about God's glory. It sounded plausible enough in Kate's front room, with a latte in your hand. But here, in the real world, he was struggling to see how any of it applied to his current tedium.

Biblical background

Read 1 Corinthians 8 v 1 – 11 v 1

- In 10 v 31 Paul tells the Christians in Corinth to do "all to the glory of God". List all the ways highlighted in this section of the letter in which the Corinthians were not doing this.
- If they were not doing all for the glory of God, what seems to have been motivating them?

In 10 v 32-33, the context of v 31, how does Paul describe what it means to do "all to the glory of God"?

Read all about it

Living for God's glory contradicts everything we've ever been taught and everything we've ever wanted to believe. I'm the center of my universe. I see everything and everyone from my perspective. So my instinct, if I think about God at all, it is to think of "Him" in relation to "me". God, for example, is just… if I can be persuaded of His justice. God is love… if He expresses it in ways acceptable to me. The net result of this heart-set is that God is brought each day to the bar of human reason and prejudice, and made to answer for His alleged failures, crimes and misdemeanors.

But if my life in every aspect is to be lived for God's glory, honor and reputation, then it is only about "me" to the extent that "I" relate to "Him". Clearly, that puts "me" well and truly in my place. Of course, the gospel assures us that there's no better place to be. But still my ego kicks and screams when it's put there.

When we start with God's glory, He becomes the reference point. I only understand justice and love in relationship to Him. If my life is to be lived for His glory, then I no longer occupy the defining place in the great scheme of things. If my life is all about His glory, then His glory becomes the great, unchangeable principle against which everything is assessed.

Believe me when I say that there are few things quite so liberating!

So what does it actually mean for my life to be all about God's glory?

It means that the person I am, the life that I live, the things I do, all commend God to others—both people and angels. It means I'm a trophy of His grace. There's no other explanation for who I am and how I live except the sovereign and supernatural work of the triune God. All this means that a life lived for God's glory is a truly extraordinary life. A life that anticipates eternity.

Imagine for a moment your arrival in heaven. All the angels are lined up to welcome you, and all the saints who've gone before are ready to cheer as you walk through the gates. Those that know you have front-row seats and you instantly recognize their faces, though they're all much more attractive than you remember. The noise is deafening and the sense of coming home is almost too much to bear. At first, you think that they're there for you and in a sense they are. But then you realize that no one is patting you on the back and saying: "good job". All the cheers are for God! All the praise is directed to Him for His magnificent work of taking a broken specimen of humanity and transforming her into a breath-taking example of what grace can do. Just as no one stands in a gallery and praises the canvas and paint, so no one in heaven will look at me and praise me for what a fine job I've made of my life. It's the artist who is applauded. It is God who is praised.

If that image captures in any way something of our destiny, then we can live now in anticipation of eternity. My life is to be of such a caliber that only grace can produce it and only God receives the glory.

Let's nail that down with some specifics.

Anyone can love his friends. Only grace can produce someone who loves his enemies and seeks their good so that God gets all the honor.

Anyone can forgive one act of betrayal. Only grace can produce someone who goes on forgiving time after time so that God gets all the honor.

Anyone can dip into her purse and give coins to a beggar. Only grace can produce someone who sells her possessions and gives the proceeds to the poor so that God gets all the honor.

Anyone can expend himself on behalf of his wife. Only grace can produce a husband and wife who open their homes to the destitute and oppressed so that God gets all the honor.

I should live my life with a radical and determined intentionality that ensures that every aspect of it honors the God who made and saved me. We need to lead thought-full lives. All too often our actions and words have no explicit thought of God. The end result of living such a thought-less life is selfishness, brokenness and sin. But by grace we can live our lives with a "glory intentionality", by constantly asking ourselves: how will this glorify God?

For example, what would change if, when I was about to get involved in an argument with my wife, I thought: how will this glorify God? If God and His glory were at the forefront of my vision, then any argument between us would be impacted in a profound way.

When I'm responding to criticism: how will this glorify God?

When I'm making decisions: how will this glorify God?

When I'm disciplining my children: how will this glorify God?

When I'm playing football: how will this glorify God?

In every aspect of my life I should be thoughtful and intentional by asking this question: how will this glorify God?

That's how radical and expansive it is. Which is why we can't put it better than the leaders of the Reformation back in the 16th century: *Soli Deo Gloria*! "Glory to God alone."

Questions for reflection

Think about how this principle works out in the following situations:

- A mother faced with an obstinate two-year-old flexing his self-will
- An old person facing his sixth evening in a row alone
- A teenager coming to terms with being paralyzed
- A 26-year-old man in a church that has an average age of 68 and an average attendance of 23

- Think about the last 24 hours. In what ways have you not lived for the glory of God? If you've not already done so, spend some time asking for God's forgiveness and thanking God for His grace lavished upon you.

- In the coming week, think about how this principle works out in your life. Make it a habit to ask yourself regularly: how will this glorify God?

- Consider how you might encourage others in the coming week to live for the glory of God.

2 A LIFE FOR OTHERS

Principle

It's not about me—it's about loving God and others.

Consider this

"It's hard to believe so much could have changed in such a short time," Lou thought to herself. She tried to think back to six months ago. She was pretty sure she wouldn't have even entertained the idea back then, not even for a minute. She liked her personal space. She was happy to be with people and help out when she could, but there were times when she needed some down-time. Her home was the ideal place. Yet here she was, sitting in her kitchen, waiting for Ayisha, the refugee from northern Iraq, to arrive. A housemate! Who would have thought it? But what else could she do? The girl needed a home and she had space.

She could almost pinpoint the moment of her change of heart. It was as she listened to a talk she had downloaded on Romans 5. She began to understand the gospel in a new way. Okay, it might be a tad clichéd, but there was no other way to describe it: she had been deeply moved and had even begun to sob. The Lord just seemed so much more real to her. And she wanted to please Him. Of course she wanted to serve and bless Ayisha, but that was because she so much wanted to serve and honor her Savior.

Biblical background

Read Matthew 22 v 34-40

- How does Jesus answer the lawyer's question?
- Why do you think Jesus answers a question about the greatest commandment by highlighting two commandments (v 37-39)?
- How might the Law and the Prophets depend on these two (v 40)?

Read all about it

Self-love is big business. A well-known cosmetic company sells its products by paying beautiful celebrities to recite the company's mantra: *"Because you're worth it"*. The UK Health Service encourages self-esteem in their employees beginning to feel stress with a ten-point plan, number four being: *"Take care of yourself—you're worth it"*. Whitney Houston once sang: *"Learning to love yourself, it is the greatest love of all"*. Sorry Whitney, notwithstanding your angelic voice, I'm afraid you've missed the point. We don't need to learn to love ourselves—that comes all too naturally.

The Bible tells us that we were not made for that.

As you read through Genesis 1, it's easy to detect a rhythm and pattern to the story. Each section begins with the words: "Then God said…" and ends with the words "There was evening, and there was morning…" Day six also begins in this way, but in verse 26 the rhythm is interrupted. God begins a conversation using the words "us" and "our": "Let us make man in our image…" Man was to be the image of the complex deity that is God. That is why it was Adam and Eve together, Adam and Eve in relationship, who were made to bear God's image. It was as they loved one another, served one another and took responsibility for one another that they revealed the character of the Creator.

Although this is *implicit* in the Genesis 1 account, it becomes *explicit* in Genesis 2. The writer fills in some of the detail of the great panorama he has painted for us in the first chapter. Eve was made after Adam, but it was not merely as a supplement to him to cure his loneliness; it was as one suitable for him that he could love. When Adam, as Eve's head, loved her, and Eve, as Adam's helper, loved him, they were walking, talking, living images of the complex, inter-personal God who made them.

This is hugely significant. At a fundamental level this answers the question many of us have asked at some time: who am I and what is my life all about? If we believe the Genesis account, we no longer have to face the prospect of a mid-life crisis or fear getting lost, forever in the dark about the point of our existence. I am made to be a lover of God and others. So whether I am a preacher, a teacher, a street cleaner or an unemployed shelf-stacker, God's call on my life is to be a *lover*. In the previous chapter, we considered asking in every situation: how will this glorify God? Now the question has expanded in line with the answer of Jesus to the lawyer: how will this express love for God and others?

Can you see the far-reaching implications of this perspective? If my life is primarily about me, then Christianity is substantially less than the inside-out, upside-down revolution that Christ died to achieve. Jesus promised that the truth would set us free. In breaking the hold of sin on our lives, He has done precisely that. Loving self is the cruelest of all slaveries: it promises everything and delivers nothing. Loving God and others is the most liberating of all freedoms: it promises everything and gives us more than we can ever imagine.

There is a refreshing simplicity in this identity and purpose for living. It's in loving God and others that we bring glory to God because it's only His grace that can do this great work in us. In Genesis 3 we see the man and woman turning away from this calling. Instead of being lovers of God and others, they both became lovers of self. The Bible reveals a world full of self-lovers. Our own experience serves as a vivid illustration of this because it repeatedly reveals a heart full of self-love.

But God's grace enables me to focus on God and others. I'm released from the bondage of self-regard. I'm set free from the stifling fear of others. I'm rescued from the debilitating pursuit of selfish satisfaction. I'm set free to live the life I was made to live.

If I love others as Christ loved others, then my sense of fulfilment or comfort is irrelevant. I won't be enslaved to the opinions of others. I'm free to love them in whatever way is most appropriate. But if, instead, I love myself, then my relationship with other people will be all about how I can get them to love me more. However, if I truly love them, then—when I need to rebuke them—I'm not going to fear what they think of me or whether they'll reject me. What stops me loving others by giving a needed, gentle rebuke is self-love. Self-love isn't just silly. It's a fundamental denial of who I am as a human being made in the image of God.

Which is reason number 267 why we are thankful for transforming grace!

Questions for reflection

- Over the coming week, look for ways in which self-love is celebrated in the media or in day-to-day life. Remind yourself in those times that you have been made in the image of God and be thankful that you have been set free to love God and others.

- Consider how this love for God and others might be expressed in your relationships at home, in work and at church.

- If you are a shy person, the next time you find yourself sitting next to someone you don't know, remind yourself that God has made you to be a lover of God and others. Ask Him for the grace to express that love in the moment. If you are an outgoing person, the next time you are in a social situation and the center of attention, remind yourself that God has made you to be a lover of God and others. Ask Him for the grace to express that love in the moment.

? Think of certain relationships that you find difficult. How does this teaching help and encourage you?

3 A LIFE OF CHANGE

Principle

God is making me more like Jesus for His glory and my good.

Consider this

Here's the thing. You want to live for Jesus. You really do. You want to love, serve and please Him. But you keep getting hit by one thing after another: unemployment, bereavement, ill health, friends letting you down. You name it, and you've been slapped in the face with it.

The bottom line is you're tired of it. You know (or at least you've been told) that God is both good and sovereign. But at this precise moment, you really can't square the circle. How can He be both good and sovereign when all this garbage is getting dumped on you?

Biblical background

Read Hebrews 12 v 1-11

- Why does the author tell us to fix our eyes on Jesus (v 2)?
- How does the author understand his readers' predicament (v 5)?
- What should be our response to the Father's action in our lives? (v 9)?
- What is the purpose of this discipline (v 10-11)?

Read all about it

The wisdom that says "if something seems too good to be true, then it probably is" is often worth listening to. Of course, we should make Christianity the exception to that general rule. But it's easy to see why people dismiss faith as a crutch for the emotionally disabled or a sop thrown to those who get a raw deal out of life.

Think for a moment or two about what the gospel claims for itself. It says that God has given Himself for us in the person of Jesus Christ. Though we are hell-deserving sinners, through His death and resurrection we are forgiven, acquitted and adopted into God's family. He's now our King and High Priest, whose very presence beside His Father assures us that the seat of absolute power in the universe is, to us, a throne of infinite grace. We've been given a new heart and God Himself has taken up residence in it. Having secured us for Himself at such a price, He will never let us go but has covenanted to complete the good work He has begun. He'll bring us to glory for His glory, as we stand before Him, bearing a striking family resemblance to our elder brother, Jesus Christ.

Our salvation, from beginning to end, is a work of God. We are the beneficiaries of a plan hatched in eternity past that stretches into eternity future. The gospel tells us that God has invested everything in our salvation: His glory, His honor, His reputation, Himself. Is that cool or what? It does seem almost too good to be true, but let me reassure you it isn't. We've got God's word on it.

But before we get too comfortable, there is one aspect of God's character that we shouldn't overlook—His determination. Everywhere we look in the Bible, we find just how single-minded God is. In fact, the Bible story is essentially a story about His determination. It seems there's no length to which He won't go to make us His own. This finds its clearest expression in the cross. If you really want to know how utterly determined God is, then see what happened to God the Son at Calvary.

Which is why He's willing to use any means in my life to make me more like Jesus. For His glory and my good.

This provides a framework to understand my life in terms of both its purpose and its details. God is determined in His pursuit of my holiness. That is the great end towards which He's working. It also explains the means He employs. God is using every situation I encounter and every adversity I endure to make me more like Jesus. For His glory and my good. I find that so helpful pastorally in both my life and the lives of others.

Let's consider what this means in practice, by using Jesus as our reference point as we look at the issue of unemployment. How is losing my job going to make me more like Jesus?

Work is a complex area. For many of us, a job involves more than simply earning a living. It's often a means of status and identity. Which means that unemployment is more than losing an income, as significant as that is. The loss of a job threatens my place in the world as well as jeopardizing my future. So, painful as unemployment is, it's a significant opportunity to trust my heavenly Father. By having my security and identity taken from me, who or what else do I have in the world but God? It's as though I am stripped naked, exposed for who I really am.

In that state of extreme vulnerability, I stand where my Savior stood. Like Him, I too must learn to trust a Father who is both good and sovereign. It's through this trial that I become more like Jesus. I rediscover my identity in Him. Even if the world considers me a nobody, I retain my true identity as a rescued sinner who, by grace, is a child of God. With this identity, I'm less likely to be enticed by the status and adulation offered by the world. And that means I'm less susceptible to its threats and intimidation.

Believe me when I say that this is an altogether good thing. This is sanity when everyone around has bought into the madness and lies of career-ism.

As for loss of income, my Father has promised to supply all my needs according to His riches in Christ Jesus. I may, of course, need to downsize and downscale. That may mean losing some of the trappings of success. But travelling light on the way to glory is no bad thing. Particularly when you think that the Son of Man lived a life of relative deprivation compared to foxes! Trusting my Father and not being anxious frees me to seek first the kingdom of God and His righteousness, whatever circumstances prevail. And that, my friend, is growing more and more like Jesus.

None of this is to make light of the pain of losing your job or any other difficulty that may strike. But understanding God's great purpose for my life helps me to see the details of my life under the care of a heavenly Father. No matter how extreme my problems, there is hope and meaning because my Father is always working for my good and His glory.

This is a sweet truth: truth you can feed on and delight in; truth to nourish your soul. Too good to be true? *Too good not to be true!*

Questions for reflection

- Consider the Christians involved in your life. Pray for them and give thanks to God for the ways in which you can see God using life's circumstances to make them more like Jesus, for His glory and their good.
- Now consider your own life and thank God for those circumstances that He is using in your life to make you more like Jesus, for His glory and your good.
- Consider how you might help the following Christian friends understand how God is both sovereign and good in all of life's circumstances:
  - Someone who is chronically unwell
  - Someone who has just had a miscarriage
  - Someone who has not received any interviews for jobs they've been applying for over the last four months

4 A LIFE OF MIRACLES

Principle

The Holy Spirit changes me through the gospel.

Consider this

Two years ago, Paul had little time for addicts. He lumped them all together as self-pitying "victims", wallowing in the mess of their own making. That's why no one was more surprised than him when he offered Jake (the "recovering alcoholic") the opportunity to do an apprenticeship. Jake was the reason the church had set up a support group for families struggling with addiction in the first place. Sarah, Jake's sister, had gotten to know a few people from church and it had become obvious that the church had a responsibility to help out this family in a very practical way. There had been some resistance from a small minority—not least Paul—to this family getting "involved" with the church. But that was two years ago. You could say a lot of water had passed under the bridge since then. Paul preferred to think of it as nothing less than a miracle.

Biblical background

Read Romans 8 v 1-17

- Note down the various ways the Spirit is described in this passage.
- How many contrasts does Paul identify in verses 2-8?

- According to verse 4, what are those who live "according to the Spirit" able to do?
- In verses 9-11 who is said to "live" in believers?
- Looking at verses 12-17, what does it mean to be "led by the Spirit" in verse 14? (See Galatians 5 v 18.)
- The Spirit plays a key role in our being "in the family" (v 14-17). Why is this identity so important? (See Exodus 4 v 22-23; Mark 1 v 11; Luke 3 v 38.)

Read all about it

We have a saying that goes something like this: "*Whatever the question, the gospel is the answer*". Obviously if you wanted to know who won Wimbledon in 2003, this statement might be found wanting. But in questions about life and godliness it comes up trumps every time.

Let's try it out.

How do you encourage people to give financially? You know that manipulation is wrong and getting people to give out of guilt is always going to be short-lived. So take them to the gospel. The answer to stinginess is the good news of God's lavish generosity in Christ. Having "freely received", I am called to "freely give". In other words, the gospel sets before me a model of generosity. And it doesn't stop there because, if it did, it would be bad news indeed. But the gospel is good news because it is also the means of generosity. It's as I reflect on His extravagant grace that my heart is softened towards God and others. The gospel is not merely God's word to His world—it's God's working word to His world. The apostle Paul talks of the gospel as being "the power of God" (Romans 1 v 16).

But how does it do it? How does a word or message become a means of grace to me by actually changing me? The answer is the Holy Spirit.

There's a tendency today to highlight (or argue about) the Spirit's more apparent and spectacular work. This focus has come at a price: namely, a failure to appreciate what we mistakenly consider His more "mundane" work.

Part of the reason for this is a misunderstanding of what "miraculous" means. Ask people to give an example of a miracle, and they will probably talk about somebody coming back from the dead or being healed from an incurable disease. Both events could, of course, rightly be called a "miracle". They would also be very exciting and very good news. But I like the following definition of a miracle: "a welcome event that is not explicable by natural or scientific laws." This broadens the category. So a resurrection is a miracle because it's inexplicable. But so too is the stingy becoming generous, the mean becoming kind, the selfish altruistic, the harsh gentle, the stubborn flexible and the proud humble.

Between us, we authors have over fifty years' experience of Christian ministry. Much has been learned in that time, not least our inability to change hearts. We can cajole, exhort, persuade, reason, argue and nag. Some of that has even been known to bring about a change of behavior. But it has never brought about a change of heart. Why? Because that work is the right and responsibilty of the Holy Spirit.

Throughout the Bible, the Holy Spirit is spoken of as the giver of life. He is the one who convicts of sin and He is the creator of saving faith. He alone is able to open blind eyes so they can see the beauty of Christ. He alone can give new hearts to sinners so they turn to Christ.

There is no spiritual life without the Holy Spirit. Which is why He is just as crucial in the task of growing me as a Christian as He is in making me a Christian. The primary means through which He works is the word of God, of which He is the author. Understanding the relationship between the Bible and the Holy Spirit is important. Not least because we often make the mistake of setting them against each other. But the Bible is never a dead letter; the gospel of which it speaks is never lifeless truth.

In Hebrews 3 v 7 the author introduces a passage from Psalm 95 written almost a thousand years earlier. Yet look at how he introduces it: "So, as the Holy Spirit says..." The verb is in the present tense ("says") when we might have expected the past tense ("said"). But the relationship of the Spirit to the Scriptures is an intimate one: the Spirit "said" it when it was originally written but He "says" it afresh to each succeeding generation when they are confronted by the word. Because He authored the word, He still speaks through the word, which is why "the word of God is living and active" (Hebrews 4 v 12).

This has at least three major implications.

1. *The importance of constant gospel exposure*

True behavior change comes about through real heart change. So my heart needs to be exposed to the gospel so that it's changed. I need to remind myself often of the great gospel truths about who God is and what He's done in Christ. It's in the Bible that I learn what the gospel is and why it's such good news. The way to character transformation is to be immersed in the gospel so that I know, love and cherish it. I need to go over the gospel again in each and every new situation so that I "heed" its truth.

When I'm reluctant to give, I need to expose myself to the gospel of God's massive kindness so that through it the Holy Spirit will soften my heart and lengthen my arms to reach deep into my pockets.

If I'm prone to gossiping, I need to expose myself to the gospel of no condemnation so that through it the Holy Spirit will soften my heart and use my tongue to build up others.

When I find myself boasting, I need to expose myself to the gospel of undeserved favor so that through it the Holy Spirit will humble me so I give the glory to my Savior.

2. *The importance of exposing others to the gospel*

What is the best way to help someone struggling with sin? Expose them to the gospel. Remind them of Christ and His work. Tell them of the cross. Remind them of the wonderful works of God throughout history as He builds up to the coming of His Son. Read, for example, Romans 5, John 3, Colossians 2, Philippians 4, Mark 1 and watch in admiration as the Holy Spirit massages it deep into their hearts.

3. *The importance of prayer*

Change in my life and change in the lives of others is not my work, but the Spirit's work. So what option do I have, but to ask Him to do His work through His word?

I don't know about you, but this makes me breathe a sigh of relief. It takes the pressure off. I know only too well that change in my life is necessary. Which is why I'm so thankful for the Holy Spirit—the faithful companion whose great delight is to see sinners grow more like their Savior.

Questions for reflection

- What are the dangers of believing we can bring about a change of heart in ourselves and others?
- Spend some time praying to your heavenly Father, asking Him for the Holy Spirit to change your life and the lives of those around you.
- Reflect on the week that has just passed. Thank God for the "miracles" that have taken place over the week in your life and the lives of others.

PART TWO

GOSPEL CENTERED PERSPECTIVES

5 LOOK UP TO GOD

Principle

I respond to the gospel with daily repentance and faith.

Consider this

Sheila was shocked at what she had just said. At first, she couldn't believe it had come out of her mouth. Of course she had to apologize, and explain that she hadn't meant to say it and she didn't know where it had come from. Maybe from watching too much TV? Anyway, she started to stutter the apology, but it all sounded so hollow and unconvincing.

She stopped herself talking, and breathed a sigh of relief. Now was the time to put up her hands and admit her guilt. According to Jesus, her words expressed what was in her heart, which meant her sin was deeper (and so more serious) than a "slipped-out" expletive or throw-away insult. What was weird was that this came as good news to her. Shame was replaced by sorrow, explanation by repentance, and defensiveness by exhilaration.

Admitting she was a specific sinner and confessing her specific sin openly meant that the good news of the cross seemed even better news than she had ever realized.

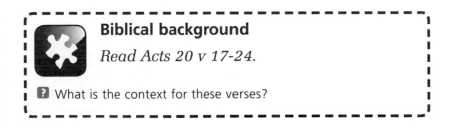

Biblical background

Read Acts 20 v 17-24.

? What is the context for these verses?

- List the various ways in which Paul describes the scope of his ministry in verses 20-21?
- Why was it important for Paul to remind his hearers in verse 21 of the nature of his message to both Jews and Greeks?
- How does Paul summarize his ministry in Ephesus at the end of verse 21?
- Why is God the focus of repentance?
- Why is the Lord Jesus Christ the focus of faith?

Read all about it

"The Holy Spirit changes me through the gospel." That's what we saw with Principle 4. So what about my role? This is one of the great, creative tensions of the Christian faith. The problem is we don't find it an easy tension to live with. We may err on the side of passivity: the Holy Spirit does it all and we do nothing—a "let go and let God" approach. Or we may err on the side of activism: the Holy Spirit is functionally absent and we do everything—a "get on and forget God" approach.

So is the answer a kind of balancing act in which the Holy Spirit and I are equal partners on a 50:50 basis? No, this is also a serious error. The gospel shows that God has given everything for our salvation and He asks for everything in return. The gospel is free, but it's not cheap. So we're not talking about a 50:50 arrangement, but a 100:100 one.

So what is our full and active involvement? Repentance and faith. This is how we first respond to the gospel and this is how we continue responding to the gospel.

Repentance

Repentance is a change of mind or heart. We realize our way of thinking and living is wrong and this leads to a new way of thinking and living. Repentance is more than a mere recognition of wrong; it's a recognition that always results in change. It's a U-turn. I'm heading in one direction. I realize it's the wrong direction. I do an about-face until I'm heading in the right direction.

The Christian life is a life of repentance. Day after day and in so many ways I see that my thoughts, words and actions are unhelpful or just plain wrong. To continue would be foolish and sinful. The Holy Spirit has convicted me and there's no option but to respond to Him, by an active turning from the sin.

Let's say Simon has problems with looking at pornography. Over the last twelve months, he's aware that it's become habitual. The Spirit convicts him of the sinfulness of his "pastime" and Simon is filled with deep sorrow at what he's been doing. If Simon then keeps visiting the offending sites, his response is mere remorse. Repentance involves Simon taking specific action to stop. It might involve moving the computer into the main room of the house or asking someone to monitor his internet activity. This isn't the full picture, but it's an important detail. It falls into the category of what the apostle Paul describes as "performing deeds appropriate to repentance" (Acts 26 v 20 NASB).

Faith

Faith is the other side of the repentance coin. They are a little bit like love and marriage which, according to the old song, "go together like a horse and carriage … you can't have one without the other." Whether that's always true of love and marriage is open to question, but it's undeniable when applied to repentance and faith. Repentance by itself is a work I do. It's possible to be persuaded that a particular act is unhelpful and so stop doing it. But when the Holy Spirit convicts of sin, He does so in relation to Christ. He turns my heart to Christ. It's in turning to Christ that I turn from my sin. Repentance recognizes that, at its core, sin is a refusal to love Christ. Gospel repentance is not just turning from sin. It's always turning to Christ because by faith we see Him as the better option. Gospel repentance is believing repentance.

This is the big issue for all of us. You'll often hear people lamenting the frenetic pace of modern life. But most of the complaints work on the assumption that we're victims of circumstances outside of our control. The reality is we spend all of our time running around trying to be our own savior—trying to give meaning to our life or trying to secure our own future. Repentance and faith involve confessing the wrongness of this kind of God-complex and instead resting in the finished and sufficient work of the only true Savior.

Let's go back to Simon and his pornography. Suppose all Simon does is stop visiting seedy sites on the internet. It's a good response, but it's not a sufficient response. A Spirit-enabled response that pleases God will involve Simon recognizing that his viewing habits are the fruit of a heart that worships itself. Every time Simon goes into his study to surf, he is in effect saying: "This is my world and I'm god". In this world of his own making, Simon rules and can do as he pleases. He has (or so he imagines) the authority to define the good life, which for him in this context is pleasure and gratification. Anyone and everyone he "meets" in this virtual world is a mere means to his ends. They exist only to serve and please him.

Repentance sees the sin for what it is. It spots the sin beneath the sin. It sees that rather than being the lover of God and others that Simon was made to be, he has chosen to be a self-lover.

Faith is the Spirit-gifted means by which Simon grasps the truth of the gospel of grace. His heart is filled with love for God and others. His life demonstrates the Spirit's work in the fruit it bears. The works of "immorality, impurity, sensuality, idolatry" and so on (Galatians 5 v 19-20 NASB) are replaced by the fruit of "love, joy, peace, patience, kindness, goodness, faithfulness, gentleness and self control" (v 22-23).

Immediately after Paul waxes eloquent about the fruit of the Spirit, he goes on to write: "those who belong to Christ Jesus have crucified the flesh with its passions and desires" (v 24). The Spirit working: the Christian working. The Spirit giving everything: the

Christian giving everything. "Since we live by the Spirit, let us keep in step with the Spirit" (v 25).

Questions for reflection

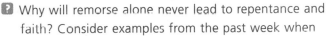

- Why will remorse alone never lead to repentance and faith? Consider examples from the past week when your response to sin has been remorse rather than repentance. Spend some time praying that the Holy Spirit will help you to be active in turning from sin.
- Is there specific action you can take to stop sinning in a certain area?
- How would you use Galatians 5 v 16-26 to counsel someone struggling with a habitual sin?

6 LOOK BACK TO THE CROSS

Principle

The cross is the foundation and pattern of my life.

Consider this

Doreen walked out of the doctor's in tears. Her illness was so frustrating. And she was worried about what others thought. They'd have a sympathetic tone when they asked why she'd missed the prayer meeting, but she knew they were disappointed with her. She guessed they thought she wasn't pulling her weight.

"Gloomy Mondays." That's what his wife called them. When Dave's sermon had gone well he was still on a high the following morning. But when it hadn't... that was a "gloomy Monday".

Kate was bitter. She'd always done her best. Always served in the church. Always avoided unbelieving boyfriends. But still God hadn't provided her with a husband. He hadn't kept His side of the bargain. In truth, she was angry with God.

What would you say to Doreen, Dave and Kate?

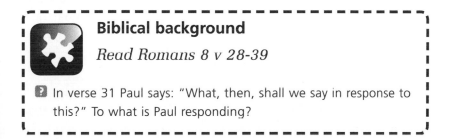

Biblical background

Read Romans 8 v 28-39

- In verse 31 Paul says: "What, then, shall we say in response to this?" To what is Paul responding?

- Paul asks the following four questions. What answers does he give?
- Who can be against us? (v 31-32)
- Who will bring any charge? (v 33)
- Who is he that condemns? (v 34)
- Who shall separate us? (v 35-37)
- How does Paul's message speak to Doreen, Dave and Kate?

Read all about it

Suppose a new Christian asks you how much they should give to the church. How would you answer? "Ten percent because that's what they did in the Old Testament"? "As much as you can afford"? "Well, this is what I do"? Or suppose a new Christian isn't giving at all. What would you say? "The church needs the funds"? "The law says you should give a tenth"? This is what Paul said: "You know the grace of our Lord Jesus Christ, that though he was rich, yet for your sakes he became poor, so that you through his poverty might become rich" (2 Corinthians 8 v 9). There's the measure and the motive of our giving: the gift of Jesus. It's the same in 1 John 3: "This is how we know what love is: Jesus Christ laid down his life for us. And we ought to lay down our lives for our brothers. If anyone has material possessions and sees his brother in need but has no pity on him, how can the love of God be in him?" (v 16-17) The cross is the model for our giving.

Or what about when someone lets you down? What's the motive and measure of our forgiveness? "Be kind and compassionate to one another, forgiving each other, just as in Christ God forgave you" (Ephesians 4 v 32).

Looking to the cross for our model

Everywhere we look in the New Testament, the cross is the motive and measure of our conduct. The cross is to shape our attitude to other Christians (Romans 15 v 7; Philippians 2 v 3-8), the opinion of unbelievers (Galatians 6 v 14), and opposition (1 Peter 4 v 12-14). It is to shape our approach to leadership (Mark 10 v 42-45) and marriage (Ephesians 5 v 25). It all goes back to the call of Jesus: "If anyone would come after me, he must deny himself and take up his cross daily and follow me" (Luke 9 v 23). The sacrificial love, self-denial and service that we see in the cross are to shape our daily lives. "Live a life of love, just as Christ loved us and gave himself up for us as a fragrant offering and sacrifice to God" (Ephesians 5 v 1-2).

It's a hard ask. It's self-denial. But Jesus says this is how you truly gain life (Mark 8 v 34-38). The way of the cross is the way of blessing (John 13 v 17). After all, it's the way of my Savior.

Looking to the cross for our acceptance

The cross is our model, but it's so much more than our model. It's our hope, our salvation, our acceptance, our life. The path of the cross will crush you if you don't also embrace the pardon of the cross. That's why we need constantly to return to the cross to rediscover acceptance, pardon, forgiveness and grace. That's why Jesus gave us the bread and wine.

In Romans 8 v 1 Paul says: "There is now no condemnation for those who are in Christ Jesus". Our sins condemn us (Romans 1-3). There's no denying it. But now there is no condemnation because Jesus Christ has redeemed us from sin and justified us before God (Romans 3 v 21-26). "For what the law was powerless to do in that it was weakened by the sinful nature, God did by sending his own Son in the likeness of sinful man to be a sin offering. And so he condemned sin in sinful man" (Romans 8 v 3). There is condemnation. God doesn't just sweep my sin under the carpet and pretend it's not there. God has condemned my sin. But He condemned my sin on the cross. Jesus the sinless one became like a sinful one because He took my sin. He died my death. He paid my penalty.

There is condemnation for Christ Jesus. But as a result "there is now no condemnation for those who are in Christ Jesus".

No condemnation. You may think of yourself as a big failure—but God doesn't. No condemnation. Other Christians may give you looks that say: "You're not pulling your weight"—but God doesn't. No condemnation. Christians need never feel condemned. The sermon may challenge you, but it cannot condemn you. Even when we do fail, even then God looks on us in Christ. He sees His beautiful, righteous Son and delights in what He sees. "The LORD your God is with you, he is mighty to save. He will take great delight in you, he will quiet you with his love, he will rejoice over you with singing" (Zephaniah 3 v 17). Always, always we can come before God with confidence and freedom, confident that we will be welcomed and forgiven. There's no need to earn approval, no need to prove ourselves, no need to perform.

Many of us know this in our heads, but still our hearts urge us to prove ourselves. Or we feel it on Sunday mornings, but still on Monday we try to find identity in our work. We can act as if we have a contract with God: He'll bless us if we serve Him. Tear up that imaginary contract! We're not God's employees. We're God's sons and daughters. Yes, we do serve God. But we don't serve God to win His blessing. It's the other way round: we're saved so we can serve Him (Ephesians 2 v 8-10). By grace we begin a relationship with our beautiful, glorious, loving heavenly Father. And as that happens, serving Him becomes its own reward.

Questions for reflection

- What will it mean for you to practice the self-denial, sacrificial love and service that we see in the cross... in the next ten minutes? Tomorrow? Next week? Next year?

- How are you following the way of the cross in the ordinary stuff of life? When the dishes need washing at home? When the chairs need putting away at church? When someone needs a visit and you're tired after a day's work and it's raining outside?

- What can you do to ensure you never stray far from the cross in your thoughts? Or in your actions?

7 LOOK AROUND AT THE CHRISTIAN COMMUNITY

Principle

Belonging to Jesus means I belong to His community.

Consider this

As the preacher finished the sermon, Susie felt a lump in her throat and she had to blink quite hard to hold back the tears. It wasn't that it was an emotional message, not by any standards. But it had clearly affected her in quite a significant way. She tried to work out what was going on. But only later, explaining things to Rod, did it begin to make any sense.

She wanted what the preacher was talking about. She wanted to be part of a community like that. She wanted to live life well and she knew she couldn't do that in isolation. But isolation actually summed up her life. Being a Christian for Susie was just about her and Jesus doing stuff together. Of course she went to church on a Sunday and she was involved in a mid-week small group. Every now and then she went to the cinema with church friends. But as she thought about the details of her life, even when she was with other people, it was as if she had been admitted to an isolation ward. Her contact with others was always behind a barrier.

"If the church is the body I heard about earlier today," she mused, "then I am an amputated little finger attached to the hand by tape!"

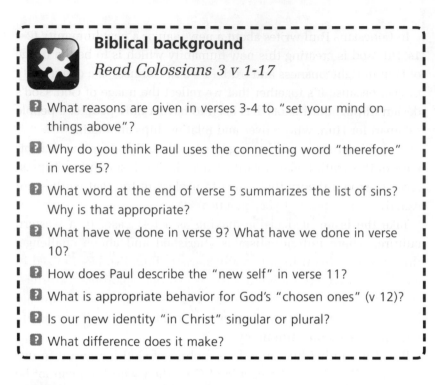

Biblical background

Read Colossians 3 v 1-17

- What reasons are given in verses 3-4 to "set your mind on things above"?
- Why do you think Paul uses the connecting word "therefore" in verse 5?
- What word at the end of verse 5 summarizes the list of sins? Why is that appropriate?
- What have we done in verse 9? What have we done in verse 10?
- How does Paul describe the "new self" in verse 11?
- What is appropriate behavior for God's "chosen ones" (v 12)?
- Is our new identity "in Christ" singular or plural?
- What difference does it make?

Read all about it

John Bunyan's *Pilgrim's Progress* is a wonderful, insightful and immensely helpful work. We've read it together as a family on more than one occasion and I'd recommend it to anyone. But, as good as it is, it only gives part of the picture. The image is of a solitary pilgrim, joined intermittently by travelling companions, making his way to the Celestial City.

I have a book on holiness which is helpful in many ways. But on its cover is a solitary figure walking across a vast expanse of sand. On the back it reads: "Holiness, the Christian's joint venture with God". The message is clear: the pursuit of holiness is a noble, but private expedition.

Neither of these examples, for all of their profound insights, gives a rounded view of the corporate dimension of a gospel-centered life. The Christian life is not less than they describe, but it is far, far more.

In Ephesians Paul writes about a new man or a new humanity (2 v 14-16). God is creating this new humanity which is to be the image of Him in righteousness and truth (4 v 24). Holiness is a community project because it's together that we reflect the image of God. God's design throughout history has been to have a holy people: a people set apart for Him, whose lives and relationships are distinctive.

Most Christians wouldn't argue with this. But does our acceptance of this truth make any difference? Isn't it just another impressive classroom theory that's next to useless in the real world—not exactly wrong, but not very practical?

Take the issue of decision-making as a test case. In a western culture, where individualism is cherished and above challenge, this is where this principle really starts to bite. I've been raised in a culture where my individual-ism is asserted vigorously, affirmed constantly and protected fiercely. The decisions I make are my decisions to make. Work, money and relationships all fall solely within my personal autonomy.

But if my individual growth as a child of God is tied up in our corporate identity as the people of God, then who I am cannot be separated from who we are. So it's impossible to make our choices and decisions without considering others. The choices I make impact the lives of my brothers and sisters. So I need to make those choices with others in mind. How is this going to affect them? How will this impact the witness of the church?

Yet in many church structures, even church leaders make decisions to move without reference to anyone in the church. The first thing the congregation hears is the announcement that the minister has accepted a "call" from another congregation. This is professionalism of the worst kind and a serious failure to model who we are in Christ.

This autonomous decision-making reveals our hearts. It shows up our self-preoccupation. God made us individuals-in-community. In the first act of rebellion in Genesis 3, the man and woman became less than they were made to be. They looked out for their own interests and blamed their sin on each other. Part of God's judgment upon them was alienation in all their relationships, not least from each other. But on the cross, Christ brought about a comprehensive reconciliation, restoring our communal identity and humanity.

So Paul says: "Do nothing out of selfish ambition or vain conceit, but in humility consider others better than yourselves. Each of you should look not only to your own interests, but also to the interests of others" (Philippians 2 v 3-4). The word "only" is not in the original text, and the words "but also" should read "but rather": "Each of you should look not to your own interests, but rather to the interests of others." It's easy to see why the translators gave in to the temptation to understate the force of Paul's exhortation.

There's no better way to affirm this radical communal focus than reminding ourselves of the one who embodied it most faithfully: "Your attitude should be the same as that of Christ Jesus: Who, being in very nature God, did not consider equality with God something to be grasped, but made himself nothing, taking the very nature of a servant, being made in human likeness. And being found in appearance as a man, he humbled himself and became obedient to death – even death on a cross!" (v 5-8)

Questions for reflection

- Think about the church that you are involved with. Do you know what it means to belong to those people that God has, in His providence, placed in your life?

- Do your non-Christian friends know the extent to which you belong to Jesus' community? Do they identify you as an isolated Christian or do they see your church as central to your identity? Is there something attractive and distinctive about the way you live as an individual-in-community?

- Consider why we're tempted to think that it's possible to belong to Jesus without belonging to His community.

- Spend some time thanking God for the provision of His people in your life and seek ways to serve Him by serving them this week.

8 LOOK FORWARD TO ETERNITY

Principle

Eternal glory offers more than this life.

Consider this

Sitting in the dentist's waiting room, Lucy flicks through *Home & Garden* magazine. She loves the photo shoots of beautifully restored homes. She dreams of a country cottage. But she and her husband have decided to serve God in the city. Looking at the antique furniture and cottage garden of some rural idyll in the country she begins to wonder whether it's worth it.

Biblical background

Read Hebrews 11 v 8-11 and 24-26; 12 v 1-3

- How did looking forward impact the actions of Abraham?
- How did looking forward impact the actions of Moses?
- How did looking forward impact the actions of Jesus?
- How should looking forward impact your actions?

Read all about it

A day is coming when Christ will be revealed in glory for all to see. A day is coming when God will recreate this sad, broken, sin-ravaged world. A day is coming when God will transform this into a world of joy, life, freedom and justice. We won't spend eternity up in heaven. Christ is coming from heaven to renew this earth. Our bodies will be raised physically, just as the body of Jesus was raised physically to live forever in a physical new earth. "Our citizenship is in heaven. And we eagerly await a Savior from there, the Lord Jesus Christ, who, by the power that enables him to bring everything under his control, will transform our lowly bodies so that they will be like his glorious body" (Philippians 3 v 20-21; see also Revelation 21 v 1-5).

If this is for real—and the Bible says this promise is trustworthy and true (Revelation 21 v 5)—then it changes everything.

But suppose for a moment it isn't true. Suppose death is the end. What kind of life would make sense? Paul tells us: "If the dead are not raised, 'Let us eat and drink, for tomorrow we die'" (1 Corinthians 15 v 32). We should live for the pleasures of this life. Hoard possessions. Pursue acclaim. Have sex whenever we can. Go on vacation. Eat and drink. For tomorrow… nothing.

But if the dead are raised, if the glory of Jesus awaits us—or the judgment of Jesus—then that changes everything. What kind of life fits with that hope? Again, Paul tells us: "And as for us, why do we endanger ourselves every hour? I die every day—I mean that, brothers—just as surely as I glory over you in Christ Jesus our Lord" (1 Corinthians 15 v 30-31). In the light of eternity, a life of daily dying to self, a life of danger, a life of sacrifice makes perfect sense. Indeed, it becomes the sensible option. Our lives are so short when compared to eternity. Sin and temptation are just a moment compared to eternity. Wealth and fame are just a moment compared to eternity. Service and suffering are just a moment compared to eternity.

So why live for the temporary glory of a broken world when you can live for the eternal glory of a renewed world?

The question is this: do our lives reflect the belief that tomorrow we die or that tomorrow we live forever? Is it obvious that your life is shaped by eternity? Are your ambitions, possessions and schedules radically different from those of your friends, colleagues and neighbors who have no eternal hope?

Consider Sue and Peter. There are so many things they miss—family and friends, cornflakes, movies, 24-hour electricity. And missionary service is demanding. Sometimes there are pangs of resentment, but they discipline their hearts. They look back to the cross. They look forward to eternity. If they think about the country they've left, then they think about returning. So instead they long "for a better country—a heavenly one" (Hebrews 11 v 15-16).

Or consider Jack. He's sitting in front of his computer. It's been a bad day. Now all he can think about is porn. It would be so easy, so secret. But he turns the computer off and phones his friend Simon. Tonight he's not going to opt for the pleasures of sin. And that's okay. After all, the pleasures of sin are for a short time and he's looking ahead to his reward (Hebrews 11 v 25-26).

Or consider Brian. A virgin on the wrong side of 30. His friends think he's crazy. He'd love a wife. But only someone who'd partner him in ministry. And that's looking less likely as every year passes. But that's okay. He's happy to put up with the disappointment and shame "for the joy set before him" (Hebrews 12 v 2).

Or consider Aisha. She parks her Fiesta alongside the Mercedes and Jags of colleagues. "When are you going to get a decent car?" they keep asking. But a flashy car doesn't do it for Aisha. It just doesn't seem important. She has better things to spend her money on—like mission and the poor. That's where her heart is. And that's okay. The treasure of heaven is better than the treasure of earth (Matthew 6 v 19-20).

Questions for reflection

- Someone once said that they try to plan their diary and finances as if they knew Christ were returning tomorrow. If your life were organized on this principle, how would it be different?
- What did you do last week for your present comfort or security? What did you do last week for God's future?
- Death separates us from every source of happiness except Jesus. Can you say with Paul that "to die is gain" (Philippians 1 v 21) because Jesus is your ultimate joy?
- John Piper says you reveal the value you put on Christ by what you are willing to risk or give up for Him. When did you last take a risk for Christ? What did you risk?
- Think about some of the big life decisions you've made—job, home, relationships. How did God's promises for the future shape those decisions?

PART THREE

GOSPEL CENTERED LIVING

9 DECISIONS

Principle

My top priority is serving Christ.

Consider this

"I want to be sure this is God's will for my life," Colin said to no one in particular. He knew it didn't contravene anything in the Bible. He'd prayed about it. Did he feel peace in his heart about it? He wasn't sure. He'd phoned his pastor who had said either option was okay. In fact his pastor hadn't seemed very interested. "Not very spiritual of him," Colin thought before checking himself.

Maybe he should open his Bible at random and point to a verse. He didn't want to step outside of God's will. But God didn't seem to be revealing His will very clearly. If only God would zap it down in some way. Colin checked his voicemail just in case. Finally he decided. He'd take the bus and not the train to work this morning.

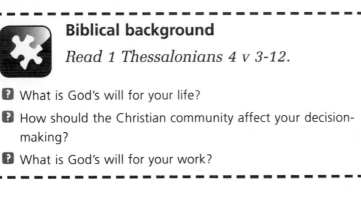

Biblical background

Read 1 Thessalonians 4 v 3-12.

- What is God's will for your life?
- How should the Christian community affect your decision-making?
- What is God's will for your work?

Read all about it

"How can I know who God wants me to marry?"

"We shouldn't just ask God to bless our plans—we should ask Him to show us His plans."

"Make sure you don't miss God's will for your life."

Statements like these appear very spiritual and often they're driven by a good desire to obey God. But their premise is unbiblical. They assume God has a specific and unique plan for the life of each Christian. God has chosen a partner, a job, and a ministry for you, it's assumed, and your job is to discover God's will so you can act upon it. The problem is God doesn't always seem to make this will very clear. Some people are left in a state of paralysis. Others look for signs or special words, while some try to read God's will from circumstances, the advise of others or a sense of peace in their hearts. In fact, the Bible never calls on Christians to seek a specific direction that is unique to them.

Decisions and the will of God

The Bible speaks of God's will in two senses.

1. **God's sovereign will.** God rules over all things so that nothing happens that He doesn't allow. In this sense, both good and evil events are part of His sovereign will. We can't know God's sovereign will for our lives ahead of time.

2. **God's moral will.** God's will also refers to the godly life that reflects God's character. It's God's will, for example, that people should love Him and love one another. God's will in this sense is universal—it's not specific to me. It's God's will that all of us should lead holy lives that bring Him glory. God's moral will for our lives isn't hidden from us because it's revealed in the Bible. We may be worried about whom we should marry or what job we should pursue, but God is more concerned that we be a godly husband or wife and a godly employee.

Decisions and the wisdom of God

The book of Proverbs repeatedly traces the link between actions and their consequences to help us understand the likely outcome of different courses of action. Wisdom is being able to make decisions with a realistic assessment of their consequences.

But true wisdom goes even deeper. "The fear of the LORD is the beginning of knowledge, but fools despise wisdom and discipline" (Proverbs 1 v 7). We like to think of ourselves as consistent, rational beings making rational decisions, but the reality is that our reason is shaped by our hearts. We find reasons for doing what we want to do. There's not necessarily anything wrong with this when the desires of our hearts are pure. The problem is that our reasoning processes are often corrupted by our sinful hearts. We all too easily "rationalize" impure desires. So true wisdom and wise decision-making begins with the fear of the LORD. It begins with a recognition of the holy God, who knows the secrets of people's hearts.

Decisions and the mission of God

Many Christians make life choices by deciding the kind of lifestyle they want. Then they choose a job to fund that lifestyle, then a home nearby, before finally choosing a local church. In fact, the choice of lifestyle is often not a conscious decision at all. Instead, our assumptions about an appropriate lifestyle are shaped by the values of the world around us. The result is leftover discipleship. My commitment to the church and Christian service comes from the leftovers of my time and money.

Instead, we need to shape our lives around a biblical vision of the good life with the enjoyment and glory of God at the center. Our top priority is serving Christ. So our decisions should begin with church and ministry, not lifestyle and job. We begin with a commitment to seek first God's kingdom. We see ourselves first and foremost as gospel ministers and members of gospel communities. Some might pursue a ministry through their careers, but they'll be intentional about that, seeing it as their ministry and not an end in itself.

This means that not only should our actions be godly, but also our motives. For example, someone could make a godly decision to pursue a certain career because they want to serve God. Another person could choose the same career, but for them it could be an ungodly decision because it reflects a desire for personal glory or greed for a high salary.

Decisions and the family of God

In our culture we've grown used to making decisions on our own, according to what suits us. "My time and my money are my affair," we say.

God, however, says "in Christ we who are many form one body, and each member belongs to all the others" (Romans 12 v 5). We are members of one body. We belong to one another. This means that we can't make decisions without regard for the Christian community. Our principle should be: we involve the Christian community in decision-making to the extent that our decisions affect the community. This doesn't mean that the community or its leaders tell people what to do in their personal lives, but it does mean that we should:

- make decisions with regard to the implications for our Christian community; and
- make significant decisions in consultation with members of our Christian community.

When someone is single, they typically decide how they spend their time and money without regard to anyone else. When they get married, everything changes. When asked to go for a drink after work, they think about the implications for their family. Big decisions get made in consultation with the family. The same is true for members of the Christian family. We're now members of one body. The family doesn't make decisions for us. But we make decisions with our family and in the light of our membership of that family.

God doesn't zap down every decision for us as we move through life. God may speak to us through His word and by His Spirit (see, for example, Acts 15 v 28; 16 v 6-7). We should be open to this without expecting it as the norm. Instead, we're free to use our God-given reason to make wise decisions as long as the options are godly, our motives are pure, the gospel is our priority and the Christian community is taken into account.

Questions for reflection

- Can you think of an example when wrong motives clouded your ability to make a godly decision?
- What is the difference between an ungodly decision and an unwise decision? Can you think of an example of both?
- Think back to a big decision you made recently: where to live, what to do with your money, what church to go to, what ministry to focus on. Jot down the stages you went through in making that decision. What were your non-negotiables in decision-making—things that you were unwilling to question? How many of those things were gospel-centered?
- Think of a decision you made recently (or a decision you're facing at the moment). How did/will your decision impact your church community? How did/will you take the church community into account in making the decision? How is/was the church community involved in your decision-making?

10 RELATIONSHIPS

Principle

I have a duty of care for others that involves taking the initiative to serve and resolve conflict.

Consider this

"Oh, I never argue," says Pat airily. "I just change the subject. Or let them have their own way. I think we should live at peace with everyone."

"Are you saying I'm a bad leader?" says Craig, emotion heavy in his voice. "Don't you trust me? I can't believe you're doing this after all I've done for you."

"I was fuming inside," recalls Ahmed. "But I stayed fairly calm, kept my voice down. I didn't say anything unkind. I wanted to say a lot more, but I didn't. I can't believe he reacted like that."

"I know I over-stepped the mark a bit," says Tracy. "But he started it. His behavior was out of line. I don't see why I should apologize. It's not my fault."

What do you make of these responses to conflict?

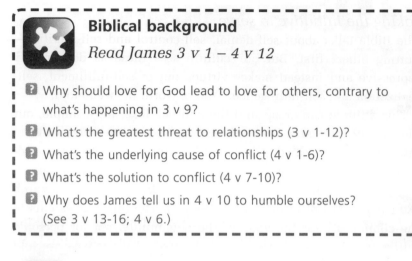

Biblical background

Read James 3 v 1 – 4 v 12

- Why should love for God lead to love for others, contrary to what's happening in 3 v 9?
- What's the greatest threat to relationships (3 v 1-12)?
- What's the underlying cause of conflict (4 v 1-6)?
- What's the solution to conflict (4 v 7-10)?
- Why does James tell us in 4 v 10 to humble ourselves? (See 3 v 13-16; 4 v 6.)

Read all about it

Our relationship to other people reveals a lot about our relationship with God.

- If you treat other people as they deserve, it might be because you think you get what you deserve from God. But if you know yourself forgiven by God, then you'll be quick to forgive others (Matthew 6 v 14-15).
- If you're indifferent towards people, it might be because you think of God as remote and unconcerned. But if you're confident of God's love, then you'll love others.
- If you're angry with people, it might be because you're angry with God. But if you feel graciously blessed beyond measure by God, then you'll be patient with other people.
- If you're selfish or self-serving, then it might be because you think you're the center of the world with God out of the picture. But if you find joy in God's glory, then you'll count it a joy to pursue that glory by serving others.

As James says, it makes no sense to praise God and curse those made in His image. Love for God is tightly linked with love for others.

Taking the initiative to serve

The Bible talks about self-denial, self-control and self-sacrifice—putting others first. But our culture sees these as dangerously repressive and instead makes virtues out of self-fulfilment, self-realization and self-indulgence. "You're worth it," we're told.

This attitude can creep into the church. Take, for example, our view of spiritual gifts. We often assume we need to work out what our gifts are so we can discover a fulfilling ministry. The Bible never tells us to do this. The point of every passage on spiritual gifts is to encourage Christians to celebrate the diversity in the church (Romans 12; 1 Corinthians 12; 1 Peter 4). The Spirit gives gifts to the community for the good of the community, not for personal fulfilment (1 Corinthians 12 v 7). Individual Christians are told humbly to serve other people and humbly to value the contributions of others. Do what needs doing. Sure, you'll get asked to do things you're good at, but don't use your "gifting" as an excuse not to serve where there's need. Be wary of people who want to "serve" the church with an up-front role, but are slow to serve the church by visiting the elderly or staying late to tidy up.

Jonathan complained of feeling tired and overworked. I tried working through his priorities with him, but it made little difference. Even after a three-month sabbatical he still felt worn out. Now he wants to "operate in his gifting". And funnily enough, his gifting doesn't include administration. He wants to do what he enjoys. Anything else makes him weary. But we can't design perfect working lives because we don't yet live in a perfect world. Most of the world spends its life in drudgery. It's arrogant to think we have a right to more. Jonathan doesn't need to find self-fulfilment. He needs to discover self-control and self-denial.

Taking the initiative to resolve conflict.

Relationships go wrong. Not particularly insightful, but all too true. Conflict is a normal part of life. And of the Christian life.

So don't suppress conflict. We suppress conflict by pretending it's not there, or giving in straight away, or personalizing issues so others give in. This doesn't mean we need to make a big deal out of every issue. Someone may slight you and you can let it go. You bear the pain internally and the matter is forgotten. If you can forget about it, then forget about it. But if it gnaws away in your mind, or it begins to affect your attitude to someone, then you need to take the initiative to address the conflict. Have a chat with the person concerned. Involve others if necessary (Matthew 18 v 16).

1. Repent

Of course, it's always someone else's fault. At least that's how it seems to us at the time. "They provoked me." "They let me down." "They started it."

But listen to James: "What causes fights and quarrels among you? Don't they come from your desires that battle within you?" (James 4 v 1) Conflict arises from the desires that battle within us. In other words, we don't get what we want. We don't get our own way. We're not treated in the way we expect. Those desires may not be bad desires—they may be good desires that have come to mean more to us than God and His glory. So when they're threatened, God's glory is not our number one concern. James calls it spiritual "adultery" (4 v 4). It means conflict can be a great opportunity to get our affections realigned to God.

Most conflicts involve fault on both sides. Where you're at fault, repent of your idolatrous desires and ask for forgiveness (don't just say "sorry" as that requires no response and so may leave the issue unresolved). Where others are at fault, make the issue not what they have done to you, but how their desires matter more to them than God. Make it an issue between them and God—don't make it all about you.

2. Forgive

The sign of a true gospel community is not a community without conflict (whose message is "we're nice people"), but a community that forgives (whose message is "God is gracious").

Forgiveness is not forgetting the incident, nor pretending it doesn't matter. Forgiveness says: "This does matter to me, but I still forgive you". This, in effect, is what God declared at the cross: "Your sin matters this much, but I still forgive you". It's an act of will that may only be the beginning of the process of healing the hurts that have been caused.

Forgiveness can be tough. We readily harbor resentment, distance ourselves and sustain hostility. But a gospel response to being wronged is a willingness to forgive. If I've been wronged by a Christian, then I've been wronged by a child of God for whom Christ has paid the penalty. By seeking to punish him or her, I'm seeking double payment. I can't exact extra payment as if Christ's death isn't enough. If I've been wronged by an unbeliever, then that person is an object of gospel witness. If they eventually do put their trust in Jesus, He will have paid for their sins on the cross. If they remain unconverted, then one day they will face God's wrath and pay themselves for all their wrongdoing. Once again, I can't exact extra payment as if God's judgment isn't enough.

- Cool off. Allow time for your emotions to calm down and use this time to pray and search your own heart.
- Talk direct. Don't moan to other people; talk to the person concerned. You may want to talk over the issue with a third party, but choose someone who'll challenge your behavior and desires.
- Listen carefully. Don't interrupt. Then check you've understood by repeating it back in your own words.
- Understand their perspective. Try to understand how you've contributed to the situation. And don't trivialize the way they feel.

- Use "I" statements instead of "you" statements. "You" statements can inflame the situation, so say: "I felt as if I was being ignored" rather than: "You were ignoring me".
- Avoid saying "but". In conflicts the word "but" will cancel what you've just said. "I appreciate your efforts, but..." = I don't appreciate your efforts!
- Do not bring up past issues. Remember, love keeps no record of wrongs (1 Corinthians 13 v 5).

Humility

Integral to healthy relationships, selfless service and resolved conflict is humility. James says: "God opposes the proud but gives grace to the humble" (James 4 v 6).

Imagine a church where everyone is trying to prove themselves or wants to be admired. Even if you don't feel proud now, you'd like to reach the point where you could be proud! If that's what you're like, you'll never serve God and you'll never serve other people. All your actions will be self-serving. Their aim will be to make you well regarded.

And pride is a fragile thing. It's fragile because it's false. We want an estimation of ourselves that doesn't fit the facts. We want to think of ourselves as good people when in fact we're deeply infected with sin. Because pride is so fragile, it needs constant reinforcement.

- We look for affirmation. We act towards others not out of selfless love, but out of a self-serving desire for their regard.
- We delight in others" failures because they bolster our standing. Last time you talked about the failures of another person, did you grieve as you talked or did you rather enjoy the conversation?
- We patronize = pride dressed up as compassion. Patronizing is what we do when we think we're better than someone, but we know we should treat them with humility.

Humility cannot be achieved! So what can we do? The great English Puritan, John Owen, may help us. He said: "There are two things that are suited to humble the souls of men, and they are, first, a due consideration of God, and then of themselves—of God, in his greatness, glory, holiness, power, majesty, and authority; of ourselves, in our mean, abject, and sinful condition." We look at ourselves through the prism of God's glory, seeing ourselves as unworthy servants of a great King. We look at other people through the prism of Christ's cross, seeing ourselves as sinners saved by grace, pointing other sinners to the fountain of grace.

Questions for reflection

- This principle talks about "taking the initiative to serve". What's the difference between simply serving and "taking the initiative to serve"? Can you think of examples?

- Look at Matthew 18 v 15-20. What "procedures" does Jesus command for dealing with conflict? Read Matthew 18 v 21-35. What are the implications of this parable for inter-personal conflict?

- Think of a recent instance of conflict in your life. What happened and what was the result? To what did you attribute the conflict in the heat of the moment? What was going on in your heart? What desires were battling for control of your heart? What steps did you take to resolve the conflict? What

11 FRIENDS

Principle

My willingness to speak about Jesus arises from my delight in Jesus.

Consider this

Sarah met up with her old college friends from time to time. Although she'd been a Christian when she was a student, she'd never gotten plugged into a local church and had spent most of her time with non-Christians. Having graduated a number of years ago, the very opposite now seemed to be true. Sarah knew that the best way to love her university friends was to tell them about Jesus, but now they didn't see each other. She often struggled to know how best to fit her old friends into this new life of hers.

The idea of speaking to the guys from work about Jesus terrified Andrew. A few of them had begun to ask him questions—they said they'd noticed a difference in the way he lived his life. Yet every time he'd wanted to answer their questions, he'd chickened out at the last minute.

Biblical background

Read Colossians 1 v 13-20

- How is the kingdom described in verse 13?
- What is said to be ours in verse 14? Why is it ours?
- List all the things Paul says about Jesus in verses 15-20.
- Now read the whole book of Colossians. As you do, keep asking why Paul focuses so much attention on Jesus.

Read all about it

Evangelism is like an extreme sport for most of us: it sounds a great idea, but we don't really have the stomach for it. We admire gifted evangelists, but their abilities make us seem inadequate. Exhortations to evangelize just leave us feeling useless. Driven by guilt, we try "turning" the conversation at work around to spiritual things with horrible, crunching gear changes, or we knock on a few doors to little effect. And so we give up. Again. And feel guilty. Again.

Love Jesus

But enthusiasm for evangelism doesn't begin with evangelism at all. It begins with an enthusiasm for Jesus. My willingness to speak of Jesus arises from my delight in Jesus. People love talking about the thing they're into. Their favorite sports team. Knitting. Vintage cars. A new boyfriend. Whatever it is, they love talking about. It bubbles out of them with an infectious passion. When we're "into" Jesus, an infectious passion for Jesus bubbles out of us. To get going on evangelism, we need to rewind to some of our earlier principles—back to God and His glory, back to God's work of change in our lives, back to the welcome and grace of the cross, back to future glory. We need to get excited all over again with Jesus. We need to excite one another with the gospel day by day.

Love people

Some people love the idea of ministry. They like the idea of being a minister or missionary. But they don't really love people. They don't make good evangelists! Step one in evangelism is being passionate about Jesus. Step two is being passionate about people. Not just seeing them as evangelistic fodder or targets for gospel salvos. But friends. People to love. Love will care for all their needs—physical, social, emotional. But gospel love also recognizes our greatest need—to know God through Christ. And so true love will always want to introduce people to our greatest friend, Jesus.

Love one another

The church is not a meeting you attend or a place you enter, but a network of relationships. A community of friends. That perspective opens up exciting possibilities. Evangelism switches from "me doing the gospel thing with my friends" to "us doing the gospel thing with our friends". It's a simple transition, but it makes a world of difference. Understanding evangelism like this means I introduce my friend who's not a Christian to my friends who are Christians. My friend gets to see us loving one another, laughing and crying together, forgiving and serving, just hanging out. He sees the gospel in action and he hears the gospel as we apply it to one another. Evangelism is going on all the time and all I've done is bring my friend into a community of friends where he's going to be exposed to the gospel. "By this all men will know that you are my disciples, if you love one another" (John 13 v 35). Evangelism transforms from a big, scary monster into a cute, little puppy you want to hug!

Loved by Jesus

Simple, isn't it? Well, actually no, it isn't! Ralph Waldo Emerson, the nineteenth-century American author, writes: "The higher the style we demand of friendship, of course the less easy to establish it with flesh and blood. We walk alone in the world. Friends, such as we desire, are dreams and fables." The major obstacle to friendship is me! So what are we to do?

"My command is this: Love each other as I have loved you. Greater love has no one than this, that he lay down his life for his friends. You are my friends if you do what I command. I no longer call you servants, because a servant does not know his master"s business. Instead, I have called you friends, for everything that I learned from my Father I have made known to you' (John 15 v 12-15).

In Jesus, we have the truest of friends: the friend who laid down His life for His friends. In His life and death, I see true friendship—friendship that draws and entices, friendship that humbles and excites. I also see a friendship that calls me into the friendship with

God for which I was made. Yet for me to enjoy that friendship, a terrible price had to be paid. At the cross, the friendship that existed between Father and Son was ruptured so that our friendship could be restored. The cross turns me from my self-obsession and self-worship. The Holy Spirit comes alongside as a friend and faithfully helps me become the friend I was made to be.

So the Christian community is the *context* for evangelism and the gospel is its *content*. The more I understand Jesus as the best of all friends, the more I'll want to introduce Him to my other friends. The more my friendship with Him deepens, the more I'll speak of Him to others.

Emerson says that true friendship requires a sort of "me too" moment. You meet someone, get talking, and at some point the other person says: "Me too, that happened to me" or "Me too, I love that as well". That shared history or shared passion is the seed of true friendship. It's a connection, a moment of identification. That's how it works in the church. We talk about our Savior. We speak of His cross. We discuss what He means to us. We share our struggles and our joys. And our hearts say: "Me too!" When our friends are exposed to that, they are exposed to Christ and may also come to see Him as the best of all possible friends.

Questions for reflection

- Do you delight in Jesus? Are you known as someone who delights in Jesus?
- Keep the list of all the things Paul says about Jesus in Colossians 1 v 15-20. Look at it when you have a spare minute, and ask the Holy Spirit to help you to love your Savior more because of who He is and all that He has done.
- Think of ways to include your non-Christian friends more in the life of your Christian community and vice versa.
- Do your non-Christian friends have opportunities to see you loving your Christian brothers and sisters and being loved by them? In the words of John, are they able to recognize that you are Jesus' disciples by the love that you have for each other (John 13 v 34-35)? If not, what can you do differently?

12 HORIZONS

Principle

The gospel enlarges my horizons, giving me a concern for God's world.

Consider this

Barry had been on a foreign vacation once or twice, but he'd basically gone for the sun. Though he loved to eat Indian food, he'd always been suspicious of immigrants. And he'd never paid much interest to foreign news unless our troops were involved. What had any of it got to do with him?

But he was blown away by Sunil's visit to his church to talk about his work in India. Immediately, he'd been taken aback by Sunil's warmth. It was as if there was a bond between them. He was moved by their work with disabled children. He was excited to hear about churches being planted. He was fascinated by stories of people being set free from demonic possession.

And now Sunil had invited him to visit for a couple of weeks, to do some building work and encourage the believers. It was all a bit crazy. Was he really going to India? As a sort of missionary?

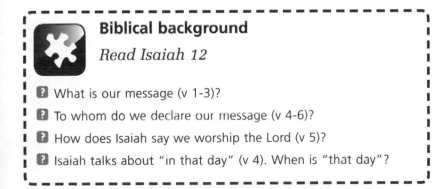

Biblical background

Read Isaiah 12

- What is our message (v 1-3)?
- To whom do we declare our message (v 4-6)?
- How does Isaiah say we worship the Lord (v 5)?
- Isaiah talks about "in that day" (v 4). When is "that day"?

Read all about it

Being a Christian broadens our horizons.

We are part of a worldwide family

When you become a Christian, you become part of a worldwide family. Strangers become brothers and sisters. You care about people you've never met. "Rejoice with those who rejoice; mourn with those who mourn," says Paul (Romans 12 v 15).

A significant feature of Paul's ministry was the collection he made among Gentile churches for the needy Christians in Jerusalem. This expressed the family relationship in which Jewish and Gentile Christians had been brought together by Christ. It was an act of practical love, but it was more than poverty relief. It had a strong, symbolic significance for the worldwide church. Paul used the collection to show that there was one worldwide church, not two (a Jewish church and a Gentile church). The collection was an expression of unity across racial, national and geographic boundaries.

The gospel both affirms and transcends cultural differences. The Bible shows that cultural diversity is part of God's intention for the human race and part of God's new humanity. Although every culture is now corrupted by sin—so that there will always be elements in any culture that Christians must challenge in the light of the gospel—cultural diversity itself is something we celebrate and encourage, part of God's grace to humanity. This means we do not make any culture absolute. We do not see our nation or ethnic group as superior. We reject all forms of racism.

The gospel is trans-cultural. It unites people of different races and cultures, so that what unites them (Christ) is more important than what divides them (cultural diversity). The church must witness to the reconciling nature of the gospel and the vision of people from every nation, tribe and tongue gathered around the throne of the lamb (Revelation 7 v 9).

Christians cannot be insular. We cannot be concerned only with our own neighborhood or nation. We have broad horizons.

We are part of a worldwide mission

The prophet Isaiah had a big vision—a vision that included the nations. God had chosen Abraham and his descendants for the sake of all nations. "All peoples on earth will be blessed through you," God had promised Abraham (Genesis 12 v 3). This promise of God shaped Isaiah's vision of the future. Isaiah looked to the day when the nations would say: "Come, let us go up to the mountain of the LORD" so they could learn God's way and enjoy His reign of peace (Isaiah 2 v 2-4). He promised a new King David, who would "raise a banner for the nations" (11 v 12). He called on God's people to sing God's praises among the nations. Worship for Isaiah was to let God's salvation "be known to all the world" (12 v 3-5). Isaiah even envisaged a day when "there will be an altar to the LORD in the heart of Egypt"—the old enemy of Israel. "Blessed be Egypt my people," God will say (19 v 19-25). Imagine how that went down among Isaiah's hearers!

Isaiah described Israel as the LORD's servant, called by God to be a light to the nations. But Israel failed in that calling and so Isaiah promises a new Servant. God's coming Servant "will bring justice to the nations ... In his law the islands will put their hope" for he will be "a light for the nations" (ESV)(42 v 1-7). Nations will come to that light (60 v 3) and the Servant will "bring [God's] salvation to the ends of the earth" (49 v 6). Matthew tells us that Jesus is this promised Servant (Matthew 12 v 15-21).

Isaiah issued an invitation on God's behalf: "Turn to me and be saved, all you ends of the earth; for I am God, and there is no other" (Isaiah 45 v 22). The book of Isaiah ends with the promise that "all mankind will come and bow down before me" (66 v 23). God will do this by sending out His people in mission to "proclaim my glory among the nations" (66 v 19).

This big vision of Isaiah for the nations shaped Paul's missionary endeavor. He often justified his ministry among the Gentiles or nations by appealing to Isaiah (Acts 28 v 23-28; Romans 9 v 27-33; 15 v 12; Galatians 4 v 27). Paul believed he was seeing in his ministry what Isaiah had promised: God was creating a people from all nations united in Christ, through the mission of the church (Romans 10 v 11-21). Isaiah talked of the nations being presented as a sacrificial offering to God (66 v 20). And this is how Paul thought of his ministry. He was made "a minister of Christ Jesus to the Gentiles with the priestly duty of proclaiming the gospel of God, so that the Gentiles might become an offering acceptable to God, sanctified by the Holy Spirit" (Romans 15 v 15-16). Romans begins with Paul's commitment "to call people from among all the Gentiles to the obedience that comes from faith" and ends with Paul glorifying God, who has revealed the gospel "so that all nations might believe and obey him" (1 v 5; 16 v 26).

Isaiah's vision for the nations should shape our missionary vision, as it did Paul's. We should share Isaiah's excitement at what God is doing through the gospel among the nations. We look forward to the time when God will "gather all nations and tongs, and they will come and see [his] glory" (Isaiah 66 v 18).

These big horizons mean Christians are committed to working for neighborhood and city renewal—redressing injustice, pursuing reconciliation and welcoming the marginalised. We can glorify God and serve others through the workplace, business, community projects, government and artistic endeavor. Above all, we litter the world with communities of light, inviting people to submit to the lordship of Jesus and enjoy His grace. Our interest in mission starts with our own neighborhood and extends to the ends of the earth.

Questions for reflection

- Remember those in prison as if you were their fellow-prisoners, and those who are ill-treated as if you yourselves were suffering" (Hebrews 13 v 3). What are you doing to express solidarity with persecuted Christians around the world?

- What difference will being part of a worldwide family make to your prayers? And to the way you watch or read the news?

- Think about "adopting" an unreached people group, a missionary family and a ministry among the poor. Make sure to get regular news about them so you can support their work through prayer and giving.

- How is your church serving God's world? How could you get involved?

13 POSSESSIONS

Principle

God gives me blessing that I might glorify Him.

Consider this

"I know the church needs cash," said Phil. "But there are loads of people who earn way more than me. Why don't you tap them for some money? It's a struggle for us as it is. Without my overtime we'd be broke."

"I don't want your money," replied Colin, his pastor. "I want your heart."

Colin looked a bit sheepish as the cameras flashed. He was receiving a big cardboard check from a local businessman—£10,000 towards their work with marginalised teenagers. As the reporters rushed off to catch their next stories, he noticed an elderly member of his congregation slip $5 into the collection box. "That poor widow has given more than anyone else," he remarked later to his assistant, Pete.

Pete sat opposite one of his youth team. "How much?" he said, trying unsuccessfully to hide the shock in his voice. "You owe $1,800? Why?" "Just stuff," was the reply. "Clothes, downloads, holiday. All the stuff everyone else has. I don't earn enough so what else was I supposed to do?"

Pete paused. *What should he say now?*

Biblical background

Read 1 Timothy 6 v 6-19

- What is the secret of contentment?
- Are possessions bad? What should be our attitude to them?
- What are the dangers of wealth?
- What does God tell the rich to do?
- How do we gain "the life that is truly life" (v 18)?

Read all about it

Nobody thinks they're rich. Most of us think the rich are people who have more than we do. But in the context of a world with over a billion people living on less than a dollar day, you are very wealthy. And Jesus says we cannot serve money and God. If you don't master money, then it will master you.

Jesus said: "The kingdom of heaven is like treasure hidden in a field. When a man found it, he hid it again, and then in his joy went and sold all he had and bought that field" (Matthew 13 v 44). This man didn't sell his possessions out of duty. He sold them "in his joy" or "in his excitement" (NLT). Do we pity the man for losing his possessions? Of course not—he was getting a much greater treasure.

In the same way, we can find giving exciting because we have a much greater treasure in view. "Don't store up treasures here on earth, where moths eat them and rust destroys them, and where thieves break in and steal. Store your treasures in heaven, where moths and rust cannot destroy, and thieves do not break in and steal." (Matthew 6 v 19-20, NLT) There is nothing intrinsically wrong with wealth. "Everything God created is good, and nothing is to be rejected if it is received with thanksgiving" (1 Timothy 4 v 4). But earthly treasure doesn't last. John Rockefeller was one of the richest men in history. After his death, someone asked his accountant: "How much money did he leave?" The accountant answered: "All of it!"

Ecclesiastes 5 (NLT) says…	*In other words…*
v10 Those who love money will never have enough. How meaningless to think that wealth brings true happiness!	The more you have, the more you want.
v11 The more you have, the more people come to help you spend it. So what good is wealth—except perhaps to watch it slip through your fingers!	The more you have, the more people will come after it.
v12 People who work hard sleep well, whether they eat little or much. But the rich seldom get a good night's sleep.	The more you have, the more you worry.
v13 There is another serious problem I have seen under the sun. Hoarding riches harms the saver.	The more you have, the more it can harm you.
v14 Money is put into risky investments that turn sour, and everything is lost. In the end, there is nothing left to pass on to one's children.	The more you have, the more you have to lose.
v15 We all come to the end of our lives as naked and empty-handed as on the day we were born. We can't take our riches with us.	The more you have, the more you'll leave behind.

Adapted from Randy Alcorn, The Treasure Principle, Multnomah.

In the film *Millions*, two boys find millions of pounds a few days before Britain converts to the euro. Soon it will be worthless. It's like that with earthly treasure—soon it will be worthless. You'd be crazy not to convert it into the currency of heaven. And the currency of heaven is good deeds, generosity, sharing: "Command them to do good, to be rich in good deeds, and to be generous and willing to share. In this way they will lay up treasure for themselves as a firm foundation for the coming age" (1 Timothy 6 v 18-19).

"Everyone who has left houses or brothers or sisters or father or mother or children or fields for my sake will receive a hundred times as much and will inherit eternal life" (Matthew 19 v 29). That's a 10,000 percent return—you won't get that from a bank! Suppose I gave you a choice: you can have a one-off gift of $10 today or, starting tomorrow, you can have $1,000 every day for the rest of your life. What would you choose? It's a no-brainer! Yet this world is full of people—and the church is full of Christians—choosing the $10 today. People live in the moment and don't look ahead to eternity.

Jesus said: "Where your treasure is, there your heart will be also" (Matthew 6 v 21). Our attitude to money is a reliable sign of where our heart is. It's the sign of true faith, love and hope. We see this again and again in the Gospels—see Luke 3 v 10-14; 16 v 9, 13-15, 19-23; 18 v 22-23; 19 v 8-9. John Wesley, the great eighteenth-century evangelist, said: "Money never stays with me. It would burn me if it did. I throw it out of my hands as soon as possible, lest it should find its way into my heart."

Jesus is saying: "Tell me how you spent your money and I'll tell you where your heart is." Think about what you've done with your money over the past month.

- If you've spent much of it on clothes, then maybe what matters to you is your outward appearance.
- If you've spent much of it on music, films or going out, then maybe what matters to you is being entertained.

- If you've carefully saved much of your money, then maybe what matters to you is security.
- If you've given much of it away, then maybe what matters to you is the true treasure of knowing Jesus.

Jesus said: "A man's life does not consist in the abundance of his possessions" (Luke 12 v 15). But the lie of our consumerist culture is that we can find life, identity and fulfilment by buying consumer goods and services. We shop for therapy. And if we don't have the money, we put it on our credit cards—we have to because our identity is at stake. Adverts promise satisfaction, but are designed to create dissatisfaction. One of the tragedies of consumerism is that people don't fully enjoy the things they acquire because they're in a perpetual state of wanting more. The gospel, in contrast, invites us to enjoy the good gifts of God's creation (1 Timothy 6 v 17).

The gospel promises much more. It promises true, lasting joy and that joy is getting God Himself. Jesus says: "I am the bread of life. He who comes to me will never go hungry, and he who believes in me will never be thirsty" (John 6 v 35). God says: "Come, all you who are thirsty, come to the waters; and you who have no money, come, buy and eat! Come, buy wine and milk without money and without cost. Why spend money on what is not bread, and your labor on what does not satisfy? Listen, listen to me, and eat what is good, and your soul will delight in the richest of fare" (Isaiah 55 v 1-2).

"Where your treasure is, there your heart will be also." Your heart follows your treasure. Giving is a liberating activity. It sets us free. It sets us free from worrying about wealth, from jealousy about wealth, and from the busyness of accumulating wealth. It sets us free from an empty way of life.

Five guidelines for giving

1. Giving should be regular, disciplined and transparent. (1 Corinthians 16 v 1-4)

2. Giving is for both rich and poor to do, in proportion to their income. (2 Corinthians 8 v 2-3, 11-12)

3. Giving should be eager and sacrificial (a tenth is a good starting point). (2 Corinthians 8 v 3-4, 9, 11)

4. Giving is a gift that helps us receive and enjoy and reflect the grace of God. (2 Corinthians 8 v 1-9)

5. Giving should go to the poor and to gospel workers. (Romans 15 v 26; Philippians 4 v 15; 1 Timothy 5 v 17-18)

Questions for reflection

- Look at advertisements in magazines or on the television. What does each one promise? How do these promises parody the promises of God?

- Look at the articles and ads in a lifestyle magazine. Think about lifestyle TV programs. How do they define the good life? What values and priorities do they represent. Look through Luke's Gospel. How does Jesus define the good life? What values and priorities does He proclaim?

- Without really thinking about it, Lucy wants a lifestyle like her friends and colleagues—a similar house, clothes, holidays, leisure activities. So she's shaped her job, location and time around those priorities. Aisha has made serving God her priority because He's her number one source of joy. She's shaped her lifestyle, job, location and time around the priorities of mission. Are you more like Lucy or Aisha?

- Look at a recent bank statement. Think back over how you've used your time in the past week. Are you laying up treasure in heaven or on earth?

14 SUFFERING

Principle

God gives me suffering that I might glorify Him.

Consider this

"Don't be so insensitive," said Jackie. "Can't you see what she's going through? No, of course not. How could you understand?"

Sheila had been ill for over a year. Much of the time she was in pain and she was left exhausted by any exertion.

Brian knew this and he was sympathetic. But lately he'd noticed her complaining more about it. When he'd talked to her about it, she'd blamed her health. "I know Christians are supposed to feel joyful, but my illness makes it different for me," she said. "When God wants me to serve Him, He'll make me well again."

Brian had decided gently to challenge Sheila's attitude. At least, he thought he'd been gentle. But Jackie clearly didn't think so!

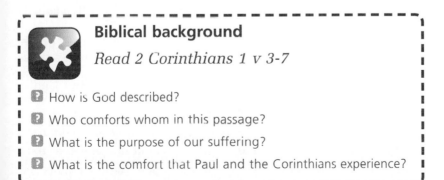

Biblical background

Read 2 Corinthians 1 v 3-7

- How is God described?
- Who comforts whom in this passage?
- What is the purpose of our suffering?
- What is the comfort that Paul and the Corinthians experience?

Read all about it

What would you say to an unbeliever who asked you about God and suffering?

Suffering may not be pointless

"A good and powerful God would and could prevent suffering so, since suffering exists, God cannot exist." So the argument goes. But this presumes that suffering serves no purpose—that it's pointless. But just because I can't see the point, it doesn't mean there isn't one. To conclude there's no point reveals an enormous leap of faith—faith in the ability of my reason to understand life.

In the Old Testament, Joseph was sold into slavery by his own brothers and then falsely imprisoned for many years. No doubt he often felt his suffering was pointless. But it meant he was in the right place at the right time to save thousands from famine and to rescue God's people. Looking back, he could say to his brothers: "You intended to harm me, but God intended it for good to accomplish what is now being done, the saving of many lives" (Genesis 50 v 20). We normally don't get the chance to look back like Joseph and see the point of our suffering. But that doesn't mean there is no point.

Job lost his property, his children and his health. He demanded answers from God and God did respond. However, He didn't come to answer Job, but to question him. "Who is this that darkens my counsel with words without knowledge? Brace yourself like a man; I will question you, and you shall answer me" (Job 38 v 2-3). Job didn't make the world, nor did he govern it. Job had no idea what the creatures "behemoth" and "leviathan" were for. The only sense they make, they make to God. The natural order and the moral order are incomprehensible to us. God is ultimately mysterious. Job didn't receive answers; he didn't get a theory. But he did receive God. "Surely I spoke of things I did not understand, things too wonderful for me to know … My ears had heard of you but now my eyes have seen you. Therefore I despise myself and repent in dust and ashes" (Job 42 v 3-6).

Suffering points to the glorious grace of God

What is the point of suffering? We don't know because we're not God. But maybe it's to demonstrate the glory of God's grace. Paul says the purpose of God's plan for the world is "that in the coming ages he might show the incomparable riches of his grace, expressed in his kindness to us in Christ Jesus" (Ephesians 2 v 7). Maybe suffering is designed to show the horrendous depth and consequences of our rebellion against God. Maybe suffering is designed to show the glorious extent and cost of our redemption by God. Maybe without suffering we would never have appreciated God's grace, nor felt secure in His love.

God has done something about suffering

Does this sound calculating on God's part, as if human suffering is a price worth paying for His own self-aggrandizement? Then remember that God Himself experienced our suffering. He died experiencing the full extent of godforsakenness: "At the ninth hour Jesus cried out in a loud voice ... 'My God, my God, why have you forsaken me?'" (Mark 15 v 34) God Himself cried out in protest against God! Why doesn't God do something about suffering? He has done something. He suffers with us

And He suffers for us. The cross is not the end of the story. Jesus rose again. His resurrection is the promise of an end to death, an end to suffering, a new beginning, a new creation, without pain, without tears. Jesus says that His return will mean "the renewal of all things" (Matthew 19 v 28). The Bible ends with this vision of the future: "Then I saw a new heaven and a new earth ... [God] will wipe every tear from their eyes. There will be no more death or mourning or crying or pain ... He who was seated on the throne said, 'I am making everything new!'" (Revelation 21 v 1-5)

Comforted, comforting

But what would you say to a Christian who asked you about God and suffering? All of this. But something else as well...

"Praise be to the God and Father of our Lord Jesus Christ, the Father of compassion and the God of all comfort, who comforts us in all our troubles, so that we can comfort those in any trouble with the comfort we ourselves have received from God. For just as the sufferings of Christ flow over into our lives, so also through Christ our comfort overflows. If we are distressed, it is for your comfort and salvation; if we are comforted, it is for your comfort, which produces in you patient endurance of the same sufferings we suffer. And our hope for you is firm, because we know that just as you share in our sufferings, so also you share in our comfort" (2 Corinthians 1 v 3-7).

We often think of suffering as our own. It makes us different. Makes us an exception. Gives us the right to be self-absorbed.

But God gives us suffering for the sake of other people. You may share a lesson you learned in your suffering. You may offer a sympathetic ear. You may speak a word of comfort from someone who's been there and found God is compassionate.

There is a "chain of comfort" here: God ▸ us ▸ others. The God of all comfort comforts us so we comfort others. And if we pass on God's comfort to others, who might they pass it on to? But if we don't pass it on, then a piece of the chain is broken.

Are you suffering in some way? Maybe there's a reason for it. Has God comforted you? Then maybe He wants you to pass that comfort on to someone else.

The "comfort" of which Paul speaks is not some sentimental "There, there, it'll be all right". It's the comfort of the gospel. It's the promise of salvation—the confident hope that through Christ there will be an end to suffering in the new creation. Pass it on.

Questions for reflection

- Retell the story of Joseph (Genesis 37; 39 - 50). How do you think Joseph felt when his brothers sold him into slavery? When Potiphar's wife falsely accused him? When the cupbearer forgot about him? What's Joseph's assessment on his life in Genesis 50 v 20?

- Think of suffering Christians who have inspired or challenged you.

- Think of people you know who are struggling. How can you comfort them with the gospel?

- How have you experienced comfort in suffering? How can you use your experience to encourage others?

FURTHER READING

Randy Alcorn, **The Treasure Principle: Unlocking the Secret of Joyful Giving**, Multnomah, 2001.

Dietrich Bonhoeffer, **The Cost of Discipleship**, SCM, 1937, 1959.

Jerry Bridges, **The Discipline of Grace**, NavPress, 1994.

Tim Chester, **You Can Change: God's Transforming Power for our Sinful Behavior and Negative Emotions**, IVP, 2008.

Tim Chester, **The Ordinary Hero: Living the Cross and Resurrection**, IVP, 2008.

C.J. Mahaney, **The Cross-Centered Life**, Multnomah, 2002.

John Piper, **Don't Waste Your Life**, Crossway, 2003.

John Stott, **The Contemporary Christian**, IVP, 1992.

Steve Timmis and Tim Chester, **The Gospel-Centered Church**, The Good Book Company, 2001.

Paul David Tripp, **A Quest for More**, New Growth Press, 2008.

Also in this series

Gospel-centered church

becoming the community God wants you to be

In *Gospel-centered church*, Steve Timmis and Tim Chester explain that gospel ministry is much more than simply evangelism. It is about shaping the whole of our church life and activities by the content and imperatives of the gospel. It is about ensuring that our church or group is motivated by and focused on the gospel, as opposed to our traditions. This workbook is designed to help clarify our thinking about how we should live our lives as the people of God.

Gospel-centered marriage

becoming the couple God wants you to be

To understand why marriages struggle—as they all do—we need to understand the nature of our sin. To make marriages work, we need to understand how to apply the truth about God and His salvation.This study guide on Christian marriage focuses on how the Gospel shapes the practical realities of everyday life. Tim Chester lifts the lid on many of the common pressure points, and shows how a proper understanding of the Gospel can shape a response.

Gospel-centered family

becoming the parents God wants you to be

Many books aim to raise up competent, balanced parents and well-trained, well-rounded children. But Tim Chester and Ed Moll focus on families growing God-knowing, Christ-confessing, grace-receiving, servant-hearted, mission-minded believers – adults and children together. In twelve concise chapters, it challenges us to become the distinctively different people that God, through His gospel, calls us to be.

Gospel-centered leadership

becoming the servant God wants you to be

Steve Timmis shares his wealth of experience and understanding in church leadership of all kinds, and strips away the modern management and marketing techniques to get back to basics. How does the gospel determine the shape, priorities and content of our leadership? Vital reading for anyone in local-church leadership of any kind.
